Simply Awesome Trips
Itineraries Ready To Go!

MW00942295

Simply Awesome Trips offers personally experienced, detailed family trip itineraries to cities and outdoor destinations in the U.S. and abroad. Our goal is to help simplify your trip planning by sharing all the details you need for an enjoyable family vacation.

Each itinerary offers favorite lodging (including Airbnb and VRBO), local food recommendations, activities that were fun for both kids and adults, labeled maps, rainy day activities, and any helpful trip tips discovered along the way--all organized into detailed, day-by-day plans.

We've put in the hours to research a fantastic trip, our own families have loved them, and we provide all you need to experience the same. You can duplicate the trip in its entirety or gather ideas for your own itinerary. Enjoy and have fun!

Happy Trails,
Amy & Amanda

www.simplyawesometrips.com

Willis Creek Slot Canyon in Grand Staircase- Escalante National Monument

Table Of Contents

Introduction

Southwest Utah has an embarrassment of riches when it comes to national parks, spectacular scenery, and outdoor activities. People spend weeks backpacking, mountain biking, horseback riding, and canyoning in this area. Even if you are not an adventure sports kind of person, there is still plenty to do. Ogle the ochre cliffs, enjoy family friendly hikes with Instagram-worthy views, and explore impossibly narrow slot canyons.

Anytime of year is a good time to visit Southwest Utah but each season can have its pros and cons. Summer is the high season, meaning all the restaurants and lodgings will be open and all of the trails are usually accessible. High season though, also means crowds so you need to book lodgings 6 months to a year in advance. High summer temperatures can make camping a sweaty business in Zion.

Fall and spring can be fun as the parks are less crowded and cooler temperatures don't force you inside in the afternoon. Spring rains and snow melt can mean that many of the slot canyons and The Narrows hike will be closed though. Winter brings the best chances for having the parks to yourself, gorgeous hikes in the snow, and cheap lodging prices. But camping will be super cold and many amenities will be closed for the season.

This guidebook focuses on Zion National Park, Bryce Canyon National Park, Kodachrome Basin State Park, and Grand Staircase- Escalante National Monument; all within an easy drive of Las Vegas and each other. We cover not just the most fun outdoor activities to do with kids, but also where to stay (whether you should be inside the park or outside, as well as camping), and the best places to eat.

We highlight the best of these parks in 7 days, but you could easily add days. As said before, these are places you could spend weeks before seeing everything. But don't try to cram it all into one week, instead take some time to savour the breathtaking views in front of you. Southwest Utah is a place that your family could return to again and again so it is okay to leave some things for next time. After all, vacations are supposed to be relaxing, not gearing up for battle!

Navajo Loop Trail in Bryce Canyon National Park

Overview Of Your 7 Days In Southwest Utah

Day 1 *Las Vegas and Zion National Park*
Arrive in Las Vegas and drive north to Utah. Explore Kolob Canyon and the Main Canyon of Zion National Park.

Day 2 *Zion National Park*
Hike the famous Narrows trail for a trek you'll never forget.

Day 3 *Zion National Park and Bryce Canyon National Park*
Spend the morning in Zion, then drive to Bryce Canyon. Stay up late to do some stargazing in one of the best places in America for it.

Day 4 *Bryce Canyon National Park*
Hike the Rim Trail at sunrise, then have a great breakfast at the Lodge. Drive the 18 mile scenic road south through the Park, stopping at several spectacular overlooks and taking a few short hikes.

Day 5 *Bryce Canyon National Park*
Do a long hike down into the canyon, getting up close to the hoodoos.

Day 6 *Grand Staircase- Escalante National Monument and Kodachrome Basin State Park*
Hike photographer's favorite Willis Slot Canyon in the morning. Explore the beautiful and crowd-free Kodachrome Basin State Park in the afternoon.

Day 7 *Drive Back to Las Vegas*

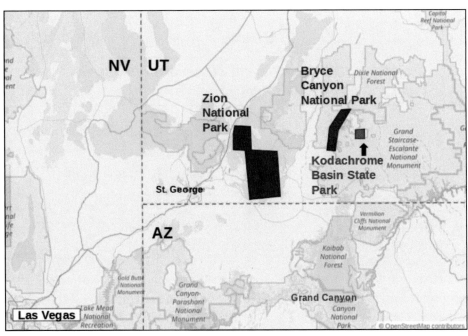

Map of 7 Day Itinerary

Hiking The Narrows in Zion National Park

Day 1

Getting to and Exploring Zion National Park

The Plan

❖ Drive north from Las Vegas to Kolob Canyons, located at the northern end of Zion National Park. (2.5 hrs/ 160 miles)

❖ Hike Timber Creek Overlook trail (1 mile RT) or Taylor Creek trail (5 miles RT) in Kolob Canyons.

❖ Drive to Springdale (1 hr/ 44 miles from Kolob Canyons) and check into your lodging in Springdale or at Zion Lodge in the park.

❖ Hike one or two easy trails in the main canyon of Zion National Park as an introduction. Have dinner at one of the excellent restaurants in Springdale.

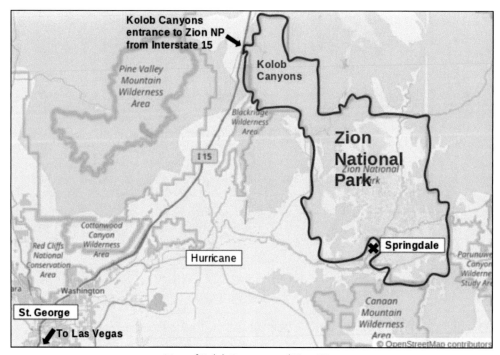

Map of Kolob Canyons and Zion NP

Morning Day 1
Arrive in Las Vegas and Drive to Kolob Canyons in Zion NP
160 miles from the airport (about 2hr 30 min driving time) *You will lose an hour driving as there is a time change between Nevada and Utah.

f you fly into Las Vegas late and need a place to stay, try the **Embassy Suites** just off the Strip. The family suite has 2 queens, sleeper sofa, 4 person table, and a huge bathroom. A large breakfast is included as well as a free beer/wine reception in the evening. There is a free shuttle to the Strip and to the airport.

Stop in St. George (30 min from Kolob Canyons) and get some sandwiches to take to the park for a picnic. **Even Stevens** sandwich shop is a good choice. You can order online for pickup to make it easy, although the restaurant has a fun interior, with cornhole and neat artwork, so it makes a nice car break if needed.

St. George is the largest town near Zion and a good place to stock up on anything you may have forgotten.

*** **Pro- Tip**- If you want any wine or beer to take to your accommodations in Utah, stop at a grocery store before you leave Las Vegas. Not only is it cheaper but anything over 3.2% alcohol has to be sold in a Utah state liquor store and they can be difficult to find. If you buy wine, don't forget a corkscrew because your lodging may not have one. (Found that out the hard way.)

Kolob Canyons
One of the lesser known parts of Zion National Park, Kolob Canyons is located an hour northwest of the main canyon and at a much higher elevation (7000 ft versus 4000 ft). Both facts make Kolob a nice alternative to the main canyon as the elevation means it is cooler, a big plus during the summer, and the distance means it has far fewer visitors.

The exit is well- marked from the interstate. Turn right into the park and you will immediately come to the **Visitor Center** on your right. You have to stop here in order to pay for the entrance pass, but it also has good bathrooms and a very small information section about the flora, fauna, and geology of the Canyons.

*** **Pro-Tip**- You can buy the Zion Park Pass ($25 per car, good for 7 days) but a better deal is the **America the Beautiful- National Parks and Federal Recreational Lands Pass** ($80, good for one year) since you are going to Bryce Canyon ($35 per car) later in the week. Saves you waiting in line to pay again and you only need to visit one more park in the next year to make it worthwhile.

From the Visitor Center, continue on the only road through Kolob Canyons. The scenic 6 mile long road has wonderful views and a couple of good hikes off of it.

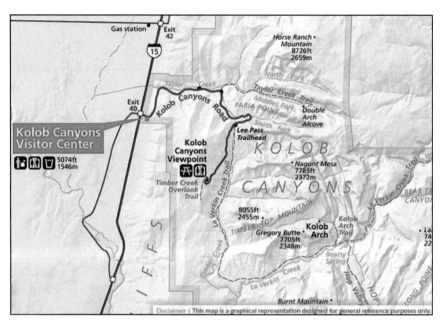

Map courtesy of the National Park Service

View from the overlook at the end of Kolob Canyons Road

Two Kid- Friendly Hikes In Kolob Canyons

1. Timber Creek Overlook Trail

This is an easy, fairly flat, 1 mile round-trip hike that leads to an overlook of Kolob Canyons. It took us about 30-45 minutes to complete and wasn't too hot, even though we were there in the early afternoon in July. This hike would also be great for sunset.

The trailhead is located at the end of Canyons Rd at the Kolob Canyons Viewpoint. You'll find vault toilets and a picnic table at the parking area. A few more picnic tables under some shady pine trees are about 150 yards down the trail.

Approaching the overlook on Timber Creek Overlook Trail

2. Taylor Creek Trail

A moderate 5 mile round- trip hike that takes approximately 3 hours. There are some old log cabins from the 1930's on the trail (Kolob Canyon was added to Zion in 1950's). At the end, you'll find the Double Arch Alcove, a cool hollowed- out arch in the canyon wall.

The trail crosses Taylor Creek about 20 times so you might need water shoes if the water is high, usually during the spring.

*** For more serious hikers- The famous Kolob Arch, one of the largest arches in North America, is in Kolob Canyons but it is a strenuous 14 mile RT hike on the La

Verkin Creek trail. If you are interested in backcountry camping though, this would be a fun 2 day hike and the campsites look really nice. Read the blog about it on the website, *Joe's Guide to Zion,* for a good, detailed description.

Lunch Day 1
Picnic in Kolob Canyons

Bring your sandwiches you bought in St. George and have a picnic at the tables on Timber Creek Overlook trail or hike 0.2 miles down to the creek on the Taylor Creek trail and find a spot along the creek.

If you don't feel like a picnic, then eat in St. George on the way to Kolob Canyons or afterwards in the towns of Hurricane or La Verkin on your way to Springdale. There is nothing around Kolob Canyons. If you want to wait until you get to Springdale, then there are plenty of restaurants there to choose from. See our recommendations in *Where To Eat in Zion NP And Springdale* on the next pages.

Early Afternoon Day 1
Drive to the Main Canyon of Zion National Park and Check into Your Lodgings

When you have seen all you want to of Kolob Canyons, drive to Springdale and the Main Canyon of Zion NP (45 min/ 38 miles from Kolob Canyons Visitor Center).

Directions: From the Kolob Canyons Visitor Center, go back out to Interstate 15 and turn left to go south. Drive 12 miles, then take exit 27 for Highway 17 South, towards Toquerville/Hurricane. After about 6 miles on Highway 17 South, turn left onto Highway 9 East to Springdale. Stay on that for about 20 miles until you come to Springdale and the entrance to Zion National Park.

General Tips For The Main Canyon Of Zion National Park

The official website is really good and covers just about everything you might need to know. In particular, check out the *Basic Information* tab and *Things To Do* tab. The *Kids and Youth* tab has information about kids activities, including the Junior Rangers and the Nature Center.

The **Nature Center** has interesting kids programs during the summer, so be sure to grab a brochure from the Visitor Center or check on the aforementioned website.

There are all kinds of Ranger-led activities every day, from hikes to nightly talks about a variety of subjects. Again, check the website or grab one of the brochures from the Visitor Center for a list. There are also bulletin boards around the Visitor Center listing daily activities. They will be the most accurate.

Unless you are staying at **Zion Lodge** (which is in the park), you cannot drive into the park March to November. You must use the shuttle bus from the Visitor Center, which runs frequently in the summer (every 7-15 min). It takes about 45 min to ride the shuttle from the Visitor Center to the Temple of Sinawava at the far end of the park, depending on how many people get on and off at each of the 8 stops the shuttle makes.

Use the Springdale shuttle to get to the Visitor Center unless you are going to the be there early because the parking lot frequently fills up by late morning. The shuttle has 9 stops throughout Springdale, including at designated public parking lots and by many of the bigger hotels, and drops off in front of Zion Outfitters, which is just across a pedestrian bridge from the Visitor Center.

*** **Pro- Tip**- Always check the website when planning your trip and right before you leave. Trails and sections of the park can be closed for maintenance, storm damage, rock slides, etc. They will post any closures at the top of almost every page on the official website. You don't want to find out the trail is closed after you have already planned your day around it.

Map of the Main Canyon of Zion NP. Map courtesy of the NPS.

Where To Stay In Or Near Zion National Park

You have three main options here: 1) Zion Lodge in the park, 2) a hotel in Springdale just outside the park, or 3), you can camp. All 3 of these are great choices, it just depends on the time of year, how many people you have in your family, and your price range.

This is our personal list of places that we have stayed in previously, were recommended by friends we trust, or we have bookmarked as possibilities for future visits.

1. Zion Lodge- The Only Hotel In The Park

Pros: It is quiet (especially March- Nov when the park is closed to private vehicles), has fantastic views, and is in close proximity to trailheads. Wildlife is commonly seen around the Lodge. Free WiFi.

Cons: It is a little expensive for what you get. Rooms start at $210 for 2 people (kids under 16 stay free). To eat anywhere besides the Lodge, you will need to take the shuttle (or drive) to Springdale. They can put a rollaway bed ($12/ night) n some rooms to sleep a max of 5 people but most rooms sleep 2-4. There are a limited number of connecting rooms which can be requested.

2. Lodgings in Springdale
Springdale is a decently- sized town, stretched along Highway 9 and boxed in by photogenic canyon walls on either side. It has hotels, restaurants, outfitters, a brewery, souvenir shops, and its own handy shuttle bus (April-Oct) to get around town. All of the places listed below are on the map on the following page.

Cable Mountain Lodge is a nice hotel within easy walking distance to the Zion Visitor Center. It has a pool and a scenic pathway along the banks of the Virgin River. We have stayed in their Wall Bed Suite with a group of 6 and were comfortable. They also have suites for 4 people. The kitchenettes are handy for whipping up breakfast. It is not a budget place as rooms start around $300 a night in the high season but we enjoyed it and would stay again.

Desert Pearl Inn is another good- looking lodge. It is a bit farther away from the entrance to Zion but the shuttle bus stops out front. Rooms can sleep 4 or 6, have a kitchenette, and there is a pool and laundry available on- site. Prices were also about $300/ night in the high season.

The **Holiday Inn Express Springdale - Zion National Park Area** and **Hampton Inn & Suites Springdale/ Zion National Park** are similar chain hotels with a pool. Both are about $270 a night during the high season and both include breakfast. The Holiday Inn Express has connecting suites but the Hampton Inn does not.

***Pro- Tip**- Anything near Zion is not cheap so if you are looking for a less expensive place, try St. George (about an hour drive from Springdale). The price drops to just over $100 for a room in a chain hotel there.

3. Camping
There are 2 main campgrounds in the main canyon of Zion-- Watchman and South. Watchman is our preference out of the two -- it is a little nicer, the campsites are slightly farther apart, and it is farther from the road than South.

You can reserve a tent site online at the Watchman Campground months ahead of time while South Campground only reserves two weeks out. If you want a site without reservations, get in line around 5am, be prepared to wait until around 9am to see if you get lucky, and cross your fingers.

Remember that it gets very hot in the summer. It was over 100℉ last time we were there in July so we booked a hotel room. If you want to camp in summer, bring a tarp for extra shade over your tent.

April and May are tent caterpillar season when the campgrounds can be absolutely covered in wriggling moth wannabes. Populations tend to be boom or bust so call ahead and see what the rangers say. You may end up booking a hotel if it's really bad. Google some pictures if you don't know what bad means.

The commercial campground in Springdale, Zion Canyon Campground and RV, is near Whiptail Grill and appears to be geared towards RVs. The tent sites are very close together. We would only stay here if nothing else was available.

If you can't get a site inside the national park, try Hi-Road Campground (formerly known as Zion RV and Campground) at the East Entrance to Zion. (See the *Map of the Main Canyon of Zion* on the previous pages for the east entrance location.) Tent sites are large and there is a general store/ pizza place across the street. Costs $49/night + tax for a tent site. It is also a slightly higher elevation than the main canyon so makes for cooler temperatures, a big plus in summer. Takes 30 min to drive to Zion Visitor Center from Hi- Road Campground.

Where To Eat In Zion And Springdale

Inside The Park
Like many national parks, Zion is not known for its food quality. Unless you bring a picnic, your only option is to eat at one of the 2 places at the Zion Lodge.

The **Red Rock Grill** is the sit down and fancier of the two choices and is open for breakfast, lunch and dinner. We have never eaten here but it looks nice if you were staying at the Lodge. Otherwise, eat at the better options in Springdale.

The **Castle Dome Cafe** is the outside snack bar at the Lodge. It is best for an ice cream, beer, or coffee break after a hike. The food is overpriced.

In Springdale
There are quite a few places to choose from so where you are staying might decide where you go. TripAdvisor and Yelp have good reviews of the options but these are our favorites.

We really like **Zion Canyon Brew Pub** and not just because of its handy location next to the pedestrian bridge to the Visitor Center. Good beer, nice view, and good burgers (meat and veggie kind) is our kind of place.

Cafe Soleil emphasizes healthy wraps, breakfast, coffee, salads, and pizza.

Whiptail Grille does Mexican fusion (think spaghetti squash enchiladas) in an old gas station, so the cool factor is high with this one. Seating is mostly outside, making it better at night than lunch in the summer. Serves local microbrews.

Zion Pizza & Noodle is a good family option as just about everybody can find something to like on a menu filled with pizza and pasta. Serves local microbrews.

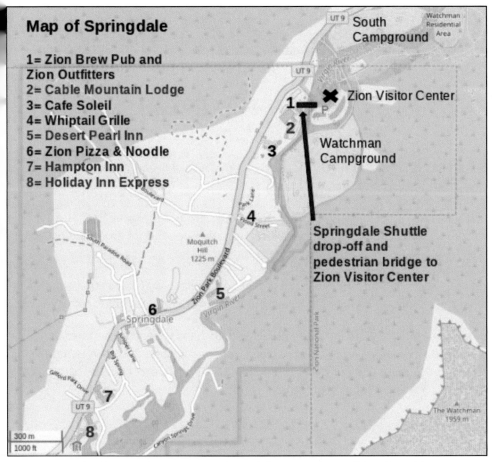

Map of Lodgings and Restaurants in Springdale. Map courtesy of OpenStreetMaps

View from the patio of the Zion Canyon Brew Pub

Late Afternoon Day 1
Pick an Activity

1. A Short Hiking Trip
Hop on the park shuttle bus and head to one of these short and easy trails. Both are marked shuttle stops.

Emerald Pools- Take an easy 1.2 miles RT paved path to the Lower Pool and its waterfall or you can hike 2.5 miles RT +400 ft to the Upper Pool. Don't expect too much from the waterfall in late summer though.

Weeping Rock - 0.5 mi RT paved trail to a huge rock face that water seeps out of. This is a great option if you want to get out of the hotel but not get too crazy.

Besides the National Park brochure (which can be hard to read sometimes online), all of these trails are covered on *Joe's Guide to Zion National Park,* a very detailed and helpful blog about all of the hikes in Zion. He also has excellent descriptions of other trails if you are looking for more strenuous hikes.

2. Tubing the Zion River
You can tube the 2 mile section of the Virgin River through Springdale from late spring through mid-summer and it is a great way to escape the afternoon heat.

Rent tubes from **Zion Outfitter** in Springdale. You should probably get life jackets for smaller children, especially if the flow rate is on the high side as the river has some surprisingly strong rapids in sections. Make sure to enquire about current conditions.

3. Go for a Bike Ride

The road through the main canyon is closed to private vehicles from March to November, meaning the only traffic to watch out for are the shuttle buses.

You can put your bike on the shuttle and hitch a ride to the Temple of Sinawava at the far end of the park. From there it is a mostly downhill, 8 mile ride back to the Visitor Center (although there is one steep uphill section at Weeping Rock). The shuttles can only hold a few bikes per shuttle though.

The paved and flat **Pa'rus trail** runs from the Visitor Center to Canyon Junction and is a great option for younger kids as it is only 1.75 miles long. It doesn't have any shade though so be careful in summer.

You can rent bikes from the **Zion Lodge** or in Springdale at **Bike Zion, Zion Cycles, Zion Outfitter**, and a few more. Biking is a popular pastime in Springdale and there are quite a few rental places. Reserve ahead if you are visiting on a weekend during the summer.

The NPS website has a good *FAQ page* about biking in Zion.

Biking during the afternoon in July and August would be an extremely hot endeavor but in the morning or evening, you should go for it. Sunset in particular is beautiful.

4. Play in Your Hotel Pool

If you are here in the afternoon during late summer, this is a smart and practical option. Save your energy for your big hike tomorrow.

*** If you happen to be in town on the 4th of July, the town has a cute festival in front of Zion Canyon Brew Pub. There is live music, good beer, and kid- friendly activities such as a dunk tank and inflatable slide. We weren't sure what to expect and ended up spending the whole afternoon.

Day 2

Hiking The Narrows in Zion National Park

A 3-10 mile RT trail that will take 2-8 hours, depending on how far you hike and how fast the river is flowing. *** Start Early!

Crossing the Virgin River while hiking The Narrows. The flow rate was 45 cfs this day.

The Narrows is one of the most iconic trails in Zion and one of our favorite trails in the world. You are basically hiking in the Virgin River for several miles as it flows through a deep canyon, which means there are photo ops worthy of National Geographic covers at every bend, but also that there are some very real dangers.

We recommend doing a little research beforehand because there are some serious warnings about hiking The Narrows. The lengthy descriptions below have everything we found useful before our hike. We gathered a ton of information because we feel more comfortable knowing exactly what to expect and what to pack for. And we just like researching things.

Despite the challenging nature of the hike and having to do some advance planning and packing, The Narrows was everyone's favorite activity in Zion. The kids are still talking about. We would put it at the top of any list of activities you want to do in the park.

Even if you have small kids, we would still say do it as you can hike as much or as little as you want. If you only make it half a mile upriver to Mystery Canyon, it is still a really cool hike that is unlike any other that we have ever done. So do some planning, be prepared, check the weather, and go for it!

Trail Description

Take the shuttle from the Visitor Center to the **Temple of Sinawava** (about 45 min) where the trailhead is located. There are good bathrooms at the shuttle stop. Use them. The shuttles start at 6am (7am in fall and spring). Be on the first ones.

The first mile is on the paved **Riverside Walk**, which is very pretty in the early morning before the hordes of people arrive. And sometimes you can see wildlife. As the name implies, it follows along the Virgin River. This is a doable trail for most anybody, including strollers and wheelchairs.

Riverside Walk ends at a pebbly beach on the Virgin River and at this point you begin your wading. After about ½ mile, you will see **Mystery Falls** on your right, so named because of the water flowing down this side of the canyon.

Riverside Walk

Keep going another mile upriver from Mystery Falls and you will enter **Wall Street.** Now the canyon walls get much more narrow and the "wow" factor amps up even more. **Orderville Canyon** is on your right and you can detour up it about a half mile to **Veiled Falls** for more fantastic photos and fun rock- scrambling.

From the junction with Orderville Canyon, you can keep going approximately another 2.5 miles up the Virgin River to **Big Spring** where day hikers (like you) must turn- around. Turning around here makes the hike about 10 miles RT.

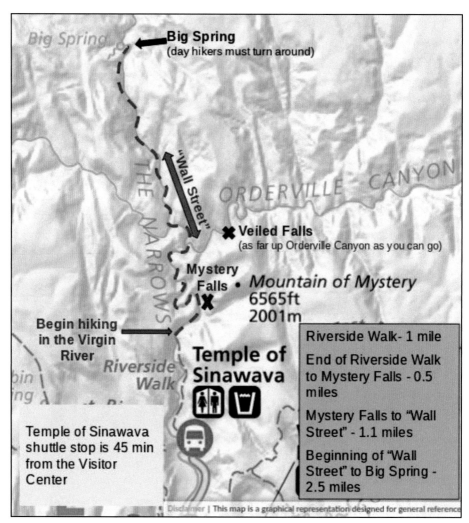

Map courtesy of the NPS with our own additions

The sun rising on Mystery Falls

We never made it all the way to Big Spring, turning around at the junction with Orderville Canyon to make our hike just under 6 miles RT, including a short detour into Orderville Canyon. It would have been about 5.2 miles RT had we not explored up Orderville Canyon.

Our not quite 6 mile round-trip hike took us about 4.5 hours with quite a few snack breaks. Our hiking speed was a pretty average speed as we were not passed by many people but also did not pass many people ourselves. We took some long breaks though, especially on the way back to let feet warm up.

To Sum up the Mileage of the Different Sections of The Narrows
- It is roughly 5 miles from beginning to end (Temple of Sinawava shuttle stop to Big Spring), not including a detour up Orderville Canyon.
- Riverside Walk - 1 mile from the shuttle stop to where the trail enters the river.
- 0.5 mile from the end of Riverside Walk to Mystery Falls.
- 1.1 miles from Mystery Falls to the beginning of Wall Street and Orderville Canyon confluence on your right
- You can explore about 0.5 miles up Orderville Canyon to Veiled Falls before seeing a NPS sign telling you to turn around.
- 2.5 miles from the beginning of Wall Street to Big Spring where day hikers must turn- around.

Things To Know About The Narrows

The Trail Is the River for Most of It and Hiking up a River is Hard
The current is against you and the footing is very slippery. Even the return trip downriver isn't a breeze as you are still searching for footing.

Be Aware of Flash Flood Risks
Check with the Wilderness Desk at the Zion Visitor Center the day before your hike. Thunderstorms miles away can lead to flash floods in the canyon so check the weather just before you leave your hotel (and leave cell service as there is none in the canyon). If the water changes from clear to muddy while you are on the trail or starts rising at all, head back immediately.

The Virgin River Is in a Canyon. There Is no "Out" Except at the Trailhead
This may seem a bit obvious but we think it stands reiterating. If you get tired, you must hike back the way you came, but more importantly, if you get caught by a flash flood, there is nowhere to go. Always check with the National Park Service for current advisories before you get on the trail.

Check the Flow Rate
There is a link to the US Geological Survey's website on the National Park Service's website page about The Narrows. Click on the link for *Current River Flow*. Scroll down for the graph showing discharge in cubic feet per second. Anything below 100 cfs is okay for hiking but look for below 50 cfs if you are hiking with children.

We hiked the trail with twin 8 year olds, a 10 year old, and a 12 year old and the flow rate was around 45 cfs (on July 5th). That was just high enough for the kids to be a challenge but still fun. We had to help them at several spots though as the water level was up to the twins' waists at times. Any higher and we would have all tired out before we got to Wall Street. The water is also cold so the level really matters if you are only 4 feet tall.

Think About Renting Gear
After much reading, we decided to skip renting canyoning shoes and just wear our Keens. While the footing wasn't bad, the temperature was. Two of the kids had uncomfortably cold feet by the end and we wish we had rented the neoprene socks, if not the shoes themselves.

Zion Outfitter in Springdale (near the pedestrian bridge to the Visitor Center) has gear, as do many of the other outfitters in town. Look online for package deals.

You Will Want Hiking Sticks
The stick helps you keep your balance in the fast moving water and gives you some support when your foot slips off a rock. And it will slip off a rock, that's a promise. Even if you don't like hiking with a stick or pole, do it for this trail.

We got to the trailhead early enough that there were a pile of very nice sticks left from the day before and the 6 of us each got one. Sticks also come with a shoe rental package if you are going to rent gear. One kid did better without his stick but the rest of us did much better with them. Err on the side of getting one.

Use the Bathrooms at the Temple of Sinawava Shuttle Stop
It is your only chance unless you pee in the river. Which everyone does. There are no secluded spots in a canyon.

The Time of Year Matters
Winter is obviously freezing but uncrowded while spring can have dangerously high water levels due to snowmelt and the trail will most likely be closed. Summer brings low water levels but also hazardous afternoon thundershowers. Fall has colder temperatures and higher water levels.

Every time of year has benefits and drawbacks. The outfitters in Springdale can set you up with dry suits if fall/ winter hiking sounds appealing.

Start Early
This is "the trail" people come to Zion to hike (along with Angel's Landing but without the nausea- inducing heights). By late morning, the first section to Mystery Falls resembles an amusement park, complete with crowds. An early start also lessens your chance of being caught in a flash flood as thunderstorms are typically in the afternoon.

We arrived at the trailhead around 7am with a full shuttle bus but the people quickly spaced out on the trail. We got some great pictures of just us and the river. By the time we got back to the trailhead around 11:30am though, we had to wind our way through the throngs of people.

Bring Dry Bags
Even if the water is low, there is a good chance you will eat it on a rock and go face first into the water with your backpack. This is one of the most gorgeous hikes we have ever done so you will want to bring your fanciest camera and you will want that dry bag for it. Snacks also taste better not soggy.

Bring Water, Food, and a Jacket

This last bit may seem unnecessary in the summer but it isn't. The sun never shone on us in the canyon until we were on the last mile out. The water is cold even in the summer and we were glad of our long- sleeved shirts and hats.

Because it is not that warm if you start early, you may not need as much water as you do in other parts of the park. We brought 1.5 liters per person and dumped 0.5L each on the way back. ***We also did not hike the whole trail.

Leave No Trace and Do Not Alter the Trail

Packing out your trash is obvious to most people but "leave no trace" also means no rock cairns, no writing your name anywhere (even in mud), and no taking a pebble home as a souvenir. Thousands of people hike this trail every year so you can see how small actions can multiply.

Orderville Canyon

Additional websites to peruse for more information about The Narrows:
Joe's Guide to Zion National Park has some good descriptions of the trail, pictures, and advice. Zion Guru Outfitters has a good description, map, and awesome graphic of how different flow rates will affect different sized hikers on their website.

Lunch Day 2

Bring a picnic to enjoy on the trail (there are occasional areas along the edge of the river that are large enough to stop and sit on the rocks out of the water).

Stop at the Castle Dome Cafe at Zion Lodge for a celebratory beer and ice cream if you had lunch on the trail.

Head back to Springdale for a well- deserved feast if you only brought granola bars for the trail. See the section on *Where to Eat In Zion And Springdale* for restaurant recommendations.

Afternoon Day 2
Optional Activities

Chill out at your lodgings with a great book for some well- deserved down time after your big hike.

Go for a bike ride or tube down the Zion River (if you aren't tired of seeing it yet).

See if there is a youth program on at the Nature Center.

Visit the **Zion Human History Museum** for its interesting 22 min video introducing the park and its history. This is a particularly good option for any summer afternoon as the museum has A/C.

Souvenir shop around Springdale.

Day 3

Morning in Zion, Afternoon in Bryce Canyon

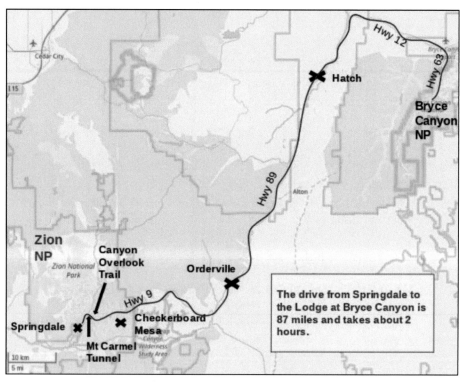

Map of Day 3. Map courtesy of OpenStreetMap

The Plan

❖ **Morning**- Check out of your lodgings and head east on Highway 9 towards Bryce Canyon. Hike the short Canyon Overlook Trail to a breathtaking overlook of Zion Canyon.

❖ **Lunch**- Stop in one of the small towns on the way to Bryce Canyon.

❖ **Afternoon/ Evening**- Check into your lodgings at Bryce Canyon National Park. Stop by the Visitor's Center to learn about the park and its famous hoodoos. Take some pictures from the rim of the canyon and stay up late to stargaze.

Morning Day 3
Short Hike and a Scenic Drive

Enjoy a more relaxing time this morning compared to yesterday. Most lodgings have an 11am checkout time so sleep in a bit and enjoy a leisurely breakfast.

After check- out, drive 30 minutes to the Canyon Overlook Trail, which is located on the other side of the Mt. Carmel Tunnel as you are heading to the East Entrance of Zion NP on Hwy 9. This drive takes much longer than the 15 minutes it should because of traffic through the tunnel.

Mt. Carmel Tunnel

The tunnel is a fantastic piece of engineering but it was built in the 1920s, long before anyone dreamed of today's behemoths driving around. It is not wide enough to let 2 RVs pass each other. Rangers must man both sides of the tunnel, halting traffic as needed. You can't stop in the tunnel but the line waiting to go through allows time to take photos of the beautiful arch you will see as you drive up to it.

When you exit the tunnel, turn into the parking lot on your immediate right. It is literally feet from the tunnel exit so be ready and looking. The Canyon Overlook trailhead is on the opposite side of the highway but it is easy to cross as there is a ranger stopping traffic and a crosswalk. If this lot is full, you'll find another small parking lot down the road on the left. From there, you walk 500ft back to the trailhead.

Canyon Overlook Trail
A easy to moderate 1 mile RT trail to a fantastic overlook of Zion Canyon

Be aware that there are a few sections of the trail that have steep drop-offs on one side and are not fenced off. The trail is fairly wide though, so the acrophobic members of the group should be okay. We took 4 kids (twin 8 year olds, a 10 year old, and a 12 year old) on the trail and had no problems. We just interspersed them between the adults and made sure there was no horsing around.

There is little shade on this trail and the rocks get very warm on summer afternoons. We hiked the trail at 1pm in early July (not the brightest idea) and we were definitely ready for some air conditioning when we got back to the car.

It is a beautiful trail though and the overlook is a huge reward for such a short hike. This is one you could over and over again.

The kids really liked this part of the Canyon Overlook Trail

The overlook at the end more than made up for some of the vertigo- inducing sections.

After you return to your car at the trailhead of Canyon Overlook Trail, continue driving on Hwy 9 about 15 min to the East Entrance of Zion National Park. Before you exit the park, you will see the Checkerboard Mesa on your right.

Checkerboard Mesa is a cool geologic formation so named because the cracks in the sandstone make it look like a checkerboard. There aren't any kid-friendly hikes through the most picturesque sections but take some photos from one of the pull-outs. If the light is good you can get some great black and white pictures.

*** If you want to do another hike or have some younger kids you did not feel comfortable taking on the Canyon Overlook Trail, try the beginning part of the East Rim Trail. Turn left for the trailhead just before the entrance gate and after you pass through the Checkerboard Mesa.

East Rim Trail is an 11 mile long, strenuous hike down into the canyon but the first few miles are fairly flat and easy hiking on the plateau. Just stop before you get to Jolley's Gulch. The website, *Joe's Guide to Zion,* has a good description.

Lunch And Afternoon Day 3
Scenic Drive and Check into Lodgings at Bryce Canyon

The Plan for the Afternoon
- ❖ Drive 80 miles (90 min) to Bryce Canyon National Park from the Canyon Overlook Trailhead
- ❖ Eat lunch on the way in the small town of Orderville or Hatch
- ❖ Check into lodgings in or near Bryce Canyon National Park
- ❖ Explore the Visitor Center and take pictures from the rim at Sunset and Sunrise Points
- ❖ Stay up to stargaze if you have the energy

Driving Instructions from Zion to Bryce Canyon
Exit Zion National Park through the East Entrance and drive 15 min until Highway 9 ends at a T-junction with Highway 89. Take a left onto Highway 89, heading north. You will drive 43 miles (45 min) until you see Highway 12 on your right.

Turn onto Highway 12 heading east and drive 17 miles (20 min) until you reach Bryce Canyon City and Highway 63 on your right. Turn right again and you are only 8 miles (15 min) from the entrance gate to Bryce Canyon National Park.

Lots of tourists travel between Zion and Bryce Canyon so there are good signs.

Highway 12 goes through a beautiful area of Dixie National Forest called Red Canyon and you will drive through 2 rock arches here. They are popular photo spots. If you want some easy hikes, stop at the Red Canyon Visitor Center on Highway 12 and pick up a pamphlet for the 0.5 mile Interpretive Trail that goes back behind the Visitor Center to see some hoodoos and learn a little about the area.

Lunch Day 3

There are some restaurants at the T-junction of Route 9 and Hwy 89. Your choices are a Subway, the Best Western restaurant, and the Golden Hills Motel restaurant. There are better choices up the road so keep going unless you are starving.

The small town of Orderville has a grocery store and a good sandwich place, **Soup Town Cafe**, along Highway 89. You'll also find **Forscher Bakery** on the north side of town that serves traditional breads and pastries flown in from Germany. Prices are on the high side though so our choice is the Soup Town Cafe unless you have a craving for German rye bread. Orderville is about 20 min from the East Entrance of Zion.

Cafe Adobe in Hatch is one of the best options for lunch (48 miles/ 1 hour driving from the East Entrance to Zion). The restaurant is on your right, just after you pass the Mormon church on the left going through Hatch on Highway 89. Cafe Adobe serves good burgers, sandwiches, and salads but no beer (too close to the church so that's a no- no in Utah as we understand). It is a fairly modest place but it tastes good and the prices are right.

***If you decide to keep driving towards Bryce Canyon for lunch, just be aware that there are not a lot of choices between Hatch and there. It is a sparsely populated area. There are a few restaurants as you get near the park and at the Bryce Canyon Lodge inside the park - see *Where to Eat In Or Near Bryce Canyon National Park* on the following pages.

ate Afternoon Day 3- Bryce Canyon National Park

Jse your America the Beautiful Pass at the entrance gate or pay $35 for a car pass good for 7 days). Check into your accommodations (see our list of suggestions on he following pages), explore around the Lodge, and get your first glimpse of the loodoos from one of the observation points along the Rim.

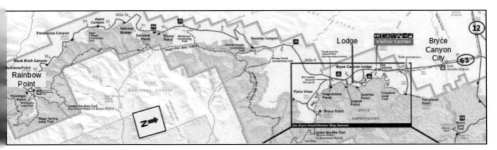

Map of Bryce Canyon National Park courtesy of the NPS with our own additions

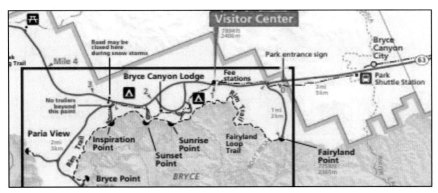

Map of Bryce Canyon National Park courtesy of the NPS

Stop in at the newly remodeled **Visitor Center** to see a 3D representation of the whole park and watch an interesting 20 minute introductory video. Get a list of ranger- guided activities. There are kids activities, geology talks, astronomy programs, and evening hikes. You can also check it out online but the Visitor Center will have the most up to date list. Look into the Junior Ranger program as most kids enjoy participating in this. The rangers at the Visitor Center are very helpful if you have questions about your hikes or the weather.

Grab dinner at one of the restaurants near your lodging or pick one from the list on the pages following - *Where To Eat In Or Near Bryce Canyon*. Finish the day by joining one of the evening ranger talks about the park and/ or stay up late to do some stargazing. Although not too late because tomorrow is an early day.

The famous hoodoos of Bryce Canyon

General Tips For Bryce Canyon National Park

Lots of people feel that Zion is the more spectacular of the two parks but don't listen to them. Between the sunrise photography of the hoodoos and the amazing night sky viewing, Bryce Canyon is all around fantastic. Don't shortchange this park when allocating your time.

Bryce is not a large park and there is only one road in and out so traffic and parking can be a hassle. But if you avoid the most popular viewpoints of Sunrise and Sunset and make an effort to be at the park early, you won't have much of a problem. We have visited in July, one of the busiest times of year, and had no problem finding parking at any spot south of Bryce Point on a weekday between 9 and 11am. There was no parking around Sunset Point though by late morning.

The Park Service operates a free, voluntary shuttle bus April- Oct that goes from Bryce Canyon City to Bryce Point and back (it does not go to the south end of the park). It has 9 stops and runs about every 15 min. The shuttle is great if you arrive midday and want to go the most popular spots. Or, if like us, you take a one- way hike and use the shuttle to get back to the car. See the website for the schedule but it basically runs 8am-8pm (6pm in spring and fall).

The biggest parking lots are by the Visitor Center. Both northbound and southbound shuttles stop there making it a convenient place to leave the car.

he rim of Bryce Canyon varies between 8,000- 9,000 feet, making it pleasant in he summer (as compared to Zion) but super cold in the winter. The canyon below hough is much warmer so dress in layers if you are hiking down into it. The altitude also means sunscreen is a necessity at any time of year. As are sunglasses.

t is possible to get altitude sickness, although rare, but many people experience shortness of breath. Small children, the elderly, or people with respiratory issues are the most likely to be afflicted, especially if they are arriving from sea level.

Plan on drinking water like you are getting paid for it. Between the altitude and the desert climate, we drank an obscene amount of water. And applied a ridiculous amount of hand lotion and chapstick. If you are from a humid climate like us, you will feel perpetually dry. Be prepared for possible nosebleeds.

Hydration backpacks are a very good idea in Bryce Canyon, for you and the kids. The adults carried Osprey daypacks with Camelbaks, which worked great, but the kids carried water bottles and it wasn't enough. While we there, we saw a kid with a small hydration backpack that was perfect. Got the details from his Mom and promptly bought one for each kid that we use all the time hiking now. Just wish we had them then. See our blog, *7 Gifts That Will Make Your Kids Want to go Outside*, to find about them.

Many commercial entities, such as lodgings, restaurants, shops, or tourist attractions, are only open seasonally (April to Oct) around Bryce Canyon. Check websites to see what's open if you are here in the offseason (generally Nov- Mar).

There is a general store in Bryce Canyon but think more tiny convenience mart rather than one- stop shopping. Bring supplies with you, especially medications, diapers (any baby supplies really), or personal hygiene products. The nearest large supermarket is in Panguitch, 40 min away, although there is a larger general store in Tropic, about 20 min away.

Print out the Map and Guide from the park website. Find it on the *Maps* page. It has a good chart of the most popular trails and the map has mileage as well. Also be sure sure to check the *Alerts* tab for any trail, lodging, or campsite closures due to fires, maintenance, storm damage, or construction. Check when you are planning your trip and then again right before you leave for changes.

***Pro- Tip**- Don't count on cell service. It was spotty at best for us once you enter the park. Download Google maps ahead of time but make sure you have a trail map as well.

Where To Stay In Or Near Bryce Canyon

There are a few great places to stay around Bryce but many choices are just okay. That's because the park is in the middle of nowhere so the choices are limited but yet receives lots of visitors so the demand is high. In the offseason you can get some good deals, although choices are even more limited.

Try to stay in the park, either at the Lodge or camping, so you can maximize your time. If that is booked, look at places in the nearby town of Tropic or camp at Kodachrome State Park as the next best choices.

This is our personal list of places that we have stayed in previously, that were recommended by friends we trust, or that we have bookmarked as possibilities for future visits.

Option 1. Stay Inside the Park - Our Recommendation*
Pros: The sunrise and the stars. The canyon faces east so watching the sun hit the hoodoos in the early morning is pretty special. The stargazing from Bryce is also outstanding but it means you will be up late at night. A short walk to and from your lodging versus a long drive could make the world of difference.

Cons: The rooms and reservable campsites book up months in advance. You must be here very early for a chance at the non- reservable campsites. Camping can be cold as freezing temperatures are possible any time of the year. There is no WiFi, TV's, or A/C in any of the rooms. (They do provide fans.) There is slow WiFi in the common areas of the Lodge, enough to check email and that's about it.

See the following pages for a specific rundown of the rooms and campsites available inside the park.

Option 2. Stay just Outside the Park in the Town of Bryce Canyon City
Pros: Close proximity to the park and a stop for the park shuttle in town. There are several okay restaurants as well as some souvenir shops.

Cons: The hotels are expensive for what you get and the campground is next to the road. Bryce Canyon City is just a collection of tourist things and not a real town.

There are 2 Best Westerns that are the best options. The **Best Western Plus Bryce Canyon Grand Hotel** has slightly higher reviews but **Best Western Plus Ruby's Inn** tends to be cheaper. Neither are great values though.

Option 3. Stay in the Nearby Town of Tropic

Pros: Tropic is cute, with a small general store and a few restaurants. Prices are better than in Bryce Canyon City.

Cons: It's a 20 min drive to Bryce and many of the choices are still rather basic.

Bryce Canyon Inn has good reviews as well as a coffee shop and pizza place on site. **Bryce Canyon Country Cabins** has log cabins that sleep 4 or 6 as well as two rental houses. Both places are on Highway 12. Look on VRBO and Airbnb for house rentals as there are a couple of decent ones in Tropic.

Option 4. Camp or Bunk in Kodachrome Basin State Park

Pros: Absolutely gorgeous, secluded campground. Unlimited hot water showers, big campsites, 2 bunkhouses that each sleep 6, and a small laundromat onsite. Great hikes just steps from the campground. Campsites reservable online. Generators only allowed from 12-4pm.

Cons: 40 min drive from Bryce Canyon. 20 min drive to the general store in Tropic.

We recommend the Basin Campground over the Bryce View Campground because it has flush toilets and showers. Both campgrounds are closed Dec- April. See Day 6 for more details about the park.

Option 5. Camp in Red Canyon Campground or King Creek Campground

Pros: Both campgrounds are in Dixie National Forest. Red Canyon is on an awesome 8.5 mile paved bike trail and there are scenic hiking trails accessible from the campground. King Creek Campground is on the Tropic Reservoir so you can canoe, swim, or fish. It also has good mountain biking trails nearby.

Cons: Both are about 30 min from Bryce Canyon (King Creek is on a gravel road). King Creek is popular with ATV people so it could be loud. Red Canyon is right off Hwy 12 so there is some road noise. Neither has reservable sites.

Option 6. Stay in the Towns of Hatch or Panguitch

Pros: More choices of all types of lodging. We found a beautiful house in Hatch big enough for 10 people that we would recommend to anyone. (VRBO #473925) Panguitch is the biggest town near Bryce Canyon so has the most choices for lodgings, restaurants, shops, etc.

Cons: Both towns are about 45 min from Bryce.

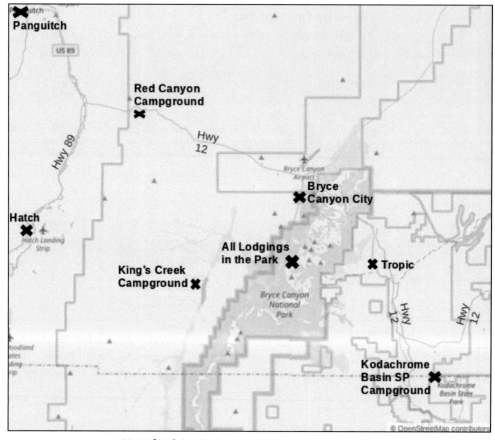

Map of Lodging Options In or Near Bryce Canyon NP

What We Did On Our Last Trip

Because we visited in early July (super busy), did not decide on this trip until about May, and had 8 people in our group, we had no chance of staying inside park although that was our first choice. We also did not want to take a gamble on first-come campsites and preferred to have a reserved spot. After exhaustively researching all the options, we ended up staying two nights at the beautiful VRBO in Hatch mentioned above and one night camping in Kodachrome Basin State Park, both of which we would do again in a heartbeat.

We have stayed in Bryce Canyon Lodge on a previous trip and loved it but you must book very early.

Rooms And Cabins In Bryce Canyon National Park

There are several types of rooms in the park, all in or next to the Bryce Canyon Lodge (see map on next page), and all are managed by Forever Resorts. Their website is easy to use and has good descriptions of the rooms. All the rooms come with a coffee maker, microwave, and mini fridge. But no A/c or WiFi.

All room prices are for 2 people per night (add $10 per person if have more than 2 adults). Kids 16 and under stay free with their adult handlers.

The Western Cabins- *Our Pick*
Rooms are $231 and sleep a max of 4 people with 2 Queen beds. The cabins are between Bryce Canyon Lodge and Sunset Point. Closed Nov- April. The cabins are in groups of 2 or 4 with shared walls so connecting doors are possible between cabins. They have a reputation for paper- thin walls so be aware.

The Sunrise and Sunset Motel Rooms
Rooms are $223/ night and have 1 King bed or 2 Queens. You can pay $15 extra for a rollaway bed in either room type to make it 3 or 5 people max. Both motels are 2 story buildings with ground floor ADA accessible rooms. Sunrise is between Bryce Canyon Lodge and Sunrise Point while Sunset is between the Lodge and Sunset Point. (Makes sense doesn't it?)

The Sunrise Motel is closed Nov- Mar and the Sunset Motel is closed Jan- Feb. The Sunset Motel is the only place open in the park during Nov and Dec and they offer a great winter deal during those months at $130/ night.

The Suites in Bryce Canyon Lodge
Suites cost $271/ night and have one bedroom (King) and a sleeper couch in the sitting area. You can sleep 5 people max if you pay $15/ night extra for a rollaway bed. Closed Nov- March. Suites are on the 2nd floor (2 flights of stairs) of the Lodge and there is no elevator.

The Studio in Bryce Canyon Lodge
The Studio costs $176/ night and has 1 Queen so sleeps a max of 2 people (room is 155 sq ft). Closed Nov- March. The Studio room is also on the 2nd floor of the Lodge with no elevator.

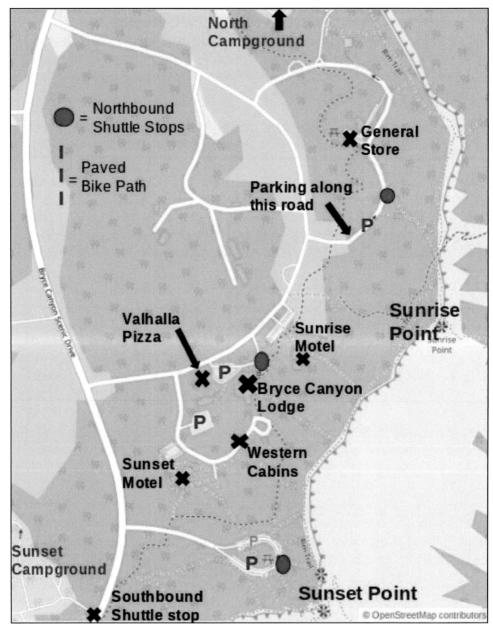

Map of Lodgings in or near the Bryce Canyon Lodge

Pro Tip - *Lodging in the park books up extremely quickly so move fast. You can book up to 13 months in advance and cancel with full refund up to 72 hours before check-in. This might one of those times to book first and make plans later.*

Camping In The National Park: North Or Sunset Campgrounds

★ Both campsites are first come- first served for 2019 as the park does construction. Check the website for updates.

Both campgrounds are open to RV's but do have dedicated, tent-only loops. Both campgrounds also have bathroom facilities with running water, but neither have showers. Both have northbound and southbound shuttle stops nearby. Sunset is closed in the winter.

The North Campground is closer to the rim and to the coin-operated showers available at the General Store so it is our first choice.

Get here early to find a spot if you don't have a reserved campsite. Definitely before noon and preferably before 10am if you are visiting in the summer.

Remember the altitude and be prepared. It can snow at any time of year and below freezing temperatures are common.

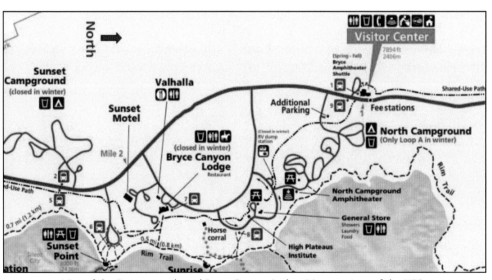

Map of the Campgrounds and Bryce Canyon Lodge. Map courtesy of the NPS

Where To Eat In Or Near Bryce Canyon

Restaurants Options Inside the National Park

The Lodge at Bryce Canyon Restaurant
This is the main dining room of the Lodge. We find it well priced and tasty, especially for a national park restaurant. Has a Kids Menu. Closed Nov- March.

Dinner can have a wait during high season as the restaurant is one of only 2 options for those staying in the park and who don't want to go to Bryce City. The breakfast buffet is reasonably priced and filling. A great option after working up an appetite on a sunrise hike, like we did.

Valhalla Pizzeria and Coffee Shop
Open for breakfast, lunch and dinner. A decent lunch option, especially if it is nice enough to sit outside. The pizzas were good enough for our hungry crew although not sure we believe the bit about them being artisanal and organic. But the price was right and they had local craft beer in cans so the parents were happy.

For a national park place, we thought it was pretty good and would go again. It is a short walk (2 min) from the shuttle stop at the Lodge to Valhalla. Only open in the summer.

The General Store
Both a small convenience mart and a small souvenir shop, the General Store has hot dogs, pizza slices, soup, and sandwiches. You can't eat inside but the porch is a great place to kick back and there are a few picnic tables around the building as well.

Located by the North Campground, the General Store is a half mile stroll from the Main Lodge on the paved bike path. It is closed January- February.

We heard that there was a tradition to stop by the General Store after a long hike to pick out an ice cream. The kids thought that was a great idea. The store also has a good selection of drinks, including single cans of craft beer, so everyone found something they wanted. Then we hung out on the porch enjoying our post-hike treats.

Restaurant Options Outside the National Park

*** Pro- Tip- Check websites if you are here in the offseason as many places are closed!

In Bryce Canyon City
There are a few places to choose from but nothing to write home about.

Ruby's Inn Cowboy Buffet and Steak Room has inexpensive, buffet food but it is popular with the tour buses so it can have a wait.

Subway is probably the best bet after Ruby's but the line can also be very long. We looked at it from the parking lot and decided to take our chances elsewhere.

Ebenezer's Barn and Grill is a dinner and show place, with a band playing old country music songs while you eat. It gets mixed reviews, basically depending on how much you like country music.

Just Outside Bryce Canyon City
on Hwy 12 heading west towards Panguitch

Foster's Family Steakhouse is 3 miles west of Bryce Canyon City and has good reviews.

Bryce Canyon Pines Restaurant is 5 miles west of Bryce Canyon CIty and has been voted the best restaurant in the area. It claims to be world famous for its pies and has an extensive list of choices, including a sour cream with raisin pie that looks enticing.

In Tropic, Utah
20 min from Bryce Canyon Lodge

This is a cute town with some good restaurants and all but one (Stone Hearth Grill) are right on Hwy 12.

Bryce Canyon Coffee Co. has good espresso, lattes, coffee, and a smattering of baked goods. It is located at the Bryce Canyon Inn where you can also find the **Pizza Place,** an inexpensive option for good pizza (they will even do gluten- free).

Rustler's Restaurant is conveniently next to Clarke's Country Market. We only stopped at the market for camping supplies but the restaurant looked nice.

Stone Hearth Grille is the only fine dining option in the area around Bryce. We never ate there as there is no entree less that $24 and we had 4 kids with us but we heard that it was very good. Only open for dinner and the only place mentioned in Tropic that is not on Hwy 12 so Google Map it before you go. Tropic isn't a big place though so not difficult to find.

I.D.K.BBQ. is actually a delicious food truck located in Cannonville (a few miles south of Tropic on Highway 12) in the parking lot of the Grand Staircase Inn. The opening hours vary based on the time of year so check their Facebook page or contact them to confirm. It is worth the effort.

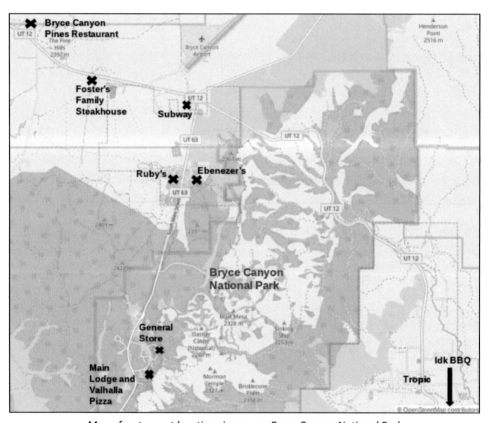

Map of restaurant locations in or near Bryce Canyon National Park

Day 4

Sunrise Hike and Scenic Drive Through the Park

The Plan

- ❖ Start early for a spectacular sunrise hike on the Rim Trail from Bryce Point to Sunset Point
- ❖ Have a hearty breakfast buffet at the Restaurant at the Lodge
- ❖ Drive 16 miles to the south end of the park at Rainbow Point and hike the short (1 mile RT) Bristlecone Pine Loop trail
- ❖ Stop at several viewpoints on the way back north through the park and have lunch at Valhalla Pizza near the Bryce Canyon Lodge
- ❖ Continue north on to Fairyland Point and then to kid-favorite Mossy Cave Trail, on the opposite side of the canyon from Fairyland Point and accessed from Hwy 12
- ❖ Have dinner in nearby Tropic, Utah

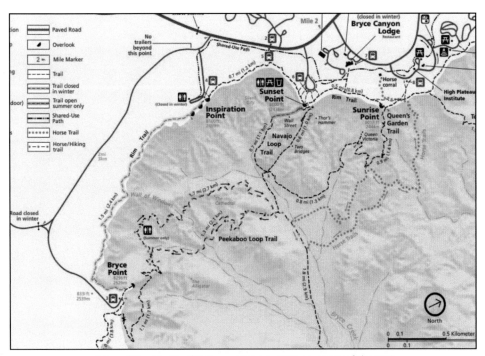

Map of the Rim Trail in Bryce Canyon. Map courtesy of the NPS

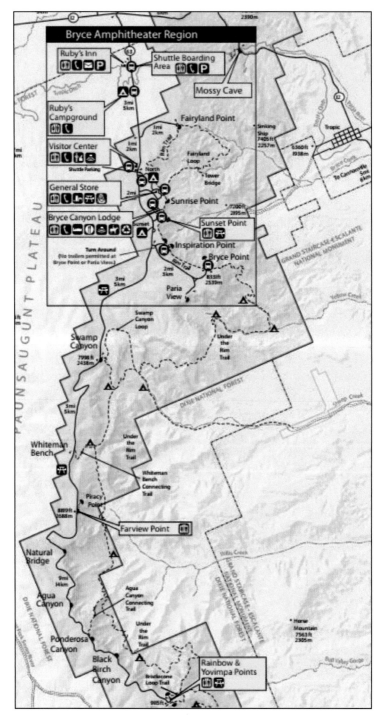

Map of the south end of Bryce Canyon, Fairyland Point, and Mossy Cave. Map courtesy of the NPS

Early Morning Day 4
Sunrise Hike Between Bryce Point and Sunset Point
Hike 2.5 miles one way, plan on around 90 minutes

The Rim Trail

The Rim Trail extends 5.5 miles from Bryce Point to Fairyland Point and has the best views in the park. The section of the trail between Bryce Point and Sunset Point is approximately 2.5 miles long and is rated easy, as you are mostly going downhill. It will take you longer to hike than you think though, because you will be stopping often for pictures. See *Map of the Rim Trail* on page 44.

If you want to start your day with more of a workout, keep hiking all the way out to Fairyland Point and then double back to the Lodge for breakfast. That will make it around 8 miles and slightly more elevation change (+/- 400ft). You will have to hike back though as there is no shuttle service to Fairyland Point.

You have to drive to Bryce Point to start this hike as the shuttles don't run early enough but don't worry, parking is fine this early in the morning. Aim to be at Bryce Point about 20 min or so before actual sunrise. It is amazing to watch the first rays peek over the mountains in the distance.

The overlook at Bryce Point is a popular spot for the sunrise and avid photographers will have set up in the best spots. We walked out to see the view and then continued down the Rim Trail a couple of hundred feet to where we had the sunrise all to ourselves.

The Rim Trail at sunrise

Sunrise over Bryce Canyon

The kids (and and most of the adults) hate getting up early but this is absolutely worth it. It was one of our best hikes ever and the hardest part was winnowing out some of the 900 pictures we took. (Only a slight exaggeration.)

Breakfast at the Restaurant at Bryce Canyon Lodge

The restaurant is a 0.25 mile walk from Sunset Point. It opens at 7am and offers a buffet and a'la carte plates. The buffet has just about everything you could want; french toast, eggs, cereal, yogurt, fruit, oatmeal, bacon, etc. and was $15/ adult and $8/ kid (12 and under), including a drink. It's awesome after a morning hike.

Retrieve the Car from Bryce Point

Catch the shuttle southbound after 8am (mid-April thru Oct) from the stop on the main road by Sunset Campground. Take the paved bike trail that runs by the Lodge to get there. It's about 0.5 miles. Don't get on the bus by the Lodge or at Sunset Point as they are northbound stops and you will have to ride all the way to Bryce City before it heads south again. See the shuttle webpage for a list of stops.

***Winter Visitors**- The Lodge is closed Nov- March so you can either walk onto the General Store (closed Jan- early March) or bring your own breakfast. There is also a good chance the Rim Trail will be closed from Bryce Point to Inspiration Point because of snow. In this case, drive to Inspiration Point and hike from there to Sunrise Point (0.5 miles beyond Sunset Point) for a 1.2 mile hike. Remember that the shuttles don't run Nov- March, so you will have to hike back to your car.

Late Morning Day 4
Scenic Drive Through Bryce Canyon National Park

Drive South to Rainbow Point and Take a Short Hike

Once you get back to your car, drive south on the main park road for 16 miles (30 min) to **Rainbow Point.** You must drive as the shuttles do not go south beyond Bryce Point. Parking is not usually an issue though in the southern sections.

Enjoy the view from the **Rainbow Point Overlook** which looks north over the entire Bryce Canyon NP. Then take the short and pretty **Bristlecone Pine Loop Trail** for an easy 1 mile RT hike. There are vault toilets by the parking area.

View north over Bryce Canyon National Park from Rainbow Point

Bristlecone Pine Loop Trail
Easy, mostly flat 1 mile loop. Expect to spend about 30 min.

According to the NPS site, some of the pine trees along this trail are 1,800 years old which is pretty mind- blowing when you think about it. The Roman Empire was falling apart, the Mayans were reaching the height of theirs, and some of these trees have been here since then. The adults thought that this was extremely cool but the kids were unimpressed. They did like the hike though.

Detour out to **Yovimpa Point** on your way back to the parking lot to see where Grand Staircase National Monument gets its name. (Hint: You can kinda see the "stairs.")

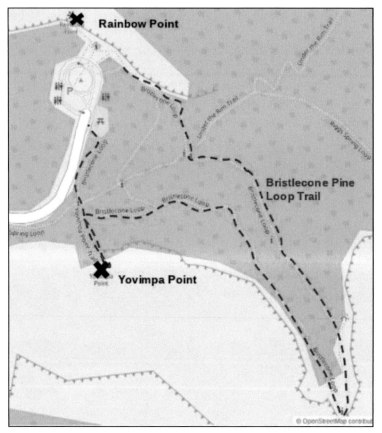

Map of Rainbow Point and Bristlecone Pine Trail

Driving Back North from Rainbow Point

On the way back towards the Lodge, stop at as many of the 6 overlooks between Rainbow and Bryce Point as you feel like. See *Map of the South End of Bryce Canyon* at the beginning of Day 4.

Each overlook has phenomenal views, but if you are time strapped, emphasize **Agua Canyon, Natural Bridge**, and **Farview Point**. Farview has a short (0.4 mile RT) hike out to Piracy Point for even better views and to get away from some of the crowds at the parking area. You'll also find vault toilets at Farview Point.

Natural Bridge

Lunch Day 4

Stop at **Valhalla Pizza** near the Lodge. Parking can be a pain in summer but it usually only takes a few drive rounds to find a spot. Valhalla has decently tasting and priced pizza as well as craft beers in cans. The outside deck is lovely if the weather is nice. See the *Map of Lodgings in or near Bryce Canyon* for location. *Valhalla is only open June through mid-September.

The sit-down restaurant at the Lodge or a hotdog/ sandwich from the General Store are your other two options.

Afternoon Day 4

Continue your Scenic Drive Through the Park and End with a Fun, Family-Friendly Hike to a Cave

After lunch, continue driving north on the main road, then take the first road to the right after the Visitor Center. Drive 1 mile to **Fairyland Point** which overlooks Fairyland Canyon.

Fairyland Canyon is the least busy part of the park. It is worth getting out and walking a short way (less than 0.5 miles) on the Fairyland Loop trail for some phenomenal views and pictures with no one in the background. If you look north, you can see the mounds left when the hoodoos eventually erode away. Eventually all of Bryce Canyon will look like this.

View from Fairyland Point

After Fairyland, hop back in the car and back out to the main road of the park. Turn right, exit the park, and go back to Highway 12. Turn right again and drive 4 miles to the Mossy Cave trailhead. Look for the small parking area on your right after you cross a small bridge over a wash. See *Map of the south end of Bryce Canyon, Fairyland Point, and Mossy Cave* at the beginning of Day 4.

Mossy Cave Trail
This is a kid-favorite because one branch of the trail ends at a shelter cave with moss growing in it and the other branch ends at a waterfall. It an easy 0.9 miles RT and the proximity to water helps keep it cool as well.

*** If you need a pick- me-up before Mossy Cave, stop first at Bryce Canyon Coffee in nearby Tropic for a caffeine jolt. It is 3.5 miles south of the trailhead on Hwy 12.

Dinner Day 4
Have dinner in Tropic at The Pizza Place at Bryce Canyon Inn, Rustler's at Clarke's Country Market, or at Stone Canyon Inn. If you want BBQ, drive south a few more miles for I.D.K. BBQ (make sure to check their Facebook page or call for hours). See *Where To Eat In Or Near Bryce Canyon* on the previous pages for more details.

If nothing in Tropic looks good, head back to the Lodge for dinner or try one of the restaurants just west of Bryce Canyon City on Highway 12.

Day 5

Long Hike Through the Hoodoos

The Plan

- ❖ **Morning** - Long hike in the morning (6.5 miles, 3- 4 hours) that combines 3 of the most popular trails in the park.

- ❖ **Lunch** - At the Lodge or Valhalla Pizza

- ❖ **Afternoon** - Relax in your lodgings so you can stay up late for some more stargazing

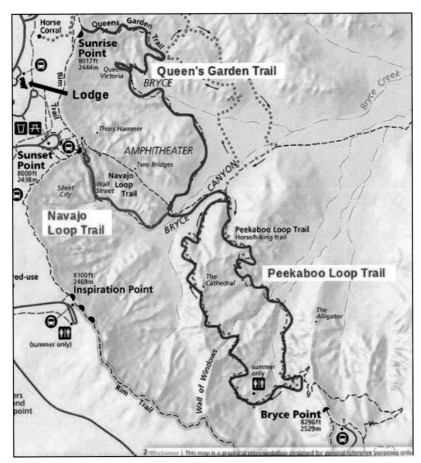

Map of the 3 Trail Combo, courtesy of the NPS with our own additions

Morning Day 5
Hike a 3 Trail Combo of Queen's Garden, Peekaboo Loop, and Navajo Loop Trails
6.5 miles total, plan on 3.5- 4.5 hours to complete

This 3 trail, figure 8 combination covers part of the canyon floor and some of the most scenic views of the hoodoos. It is 6.5 miles to complete the loop, with a long downhill at the beginning, a moderate climb between miles 2 and 3, and a steep climb at the end. The trails combine to make 6 miles plus about 0.5 miles to get to and from your car parked either at the Lodge, Sunset, or Sunrise Point.

Start early as it gets hot down in the canyon. Aim to be done by lunch, so start around 7- 9 am. In the summer, definitely start no later than 8am.

First Section- Queen's Garden Trail
About 1.8 miles, almost all downhill

Begin at Sunrise Point and start your descent into the canyon, taking lots of pictures of the spectacular hoodoos and enjoying the tunnels through them.

After just under a mile you will see a detour to your right for the Queen's Garden, a small amphitheater about 75 yards up this spur trail. The hoodoos there aren't really any different than the ones along the way so we found it kind of skippable.

Supposedly one of the hoodoos in the Queen's Garden looks like Queen Victoria sitting on a horse, which gives this amphitheater its name. We never saw anything which resembled a person (or a horse), but the kids had fun guessing.

Eventually, you will come to a junction with Navajo Loop Trail and a connector trail to Peekaboo Loop. It is decently signed so you won't miss it if you are looking.

If you are ready to bail at this point, take either side of the Navajo Loop up to Sunrise Point. We like the Wall Street side which is only 0.7 miles but climbs nearly 550ft. The Two Bridges side has similar length and elevation. If you are ready to hike on, follow the signs for Peekaboo Loop and hike the 0.2 mile connecting trail to it.

Queen's Garden Trail

Middle Section- Peekaboo Loop Trail

3 miles long, a 400ft climb in the first mile, a 200ft climb on the last mile

You can hike Peekaboo Loop either clockwise or counterclockwise. The blog *Modern Hiker* has a detailed description of the 3 trail combo and we agree with him that counter-clockwise might be better so you get the worst climb done first. His pictures and description are great if you want additional info.

Some of the best views in the park are on the western side of this trail, e.g the Wall of Windows. So despite the steep climb in parts, it is worth it. Just take it slow and drink lots of water.

After you complete the loop, hike back on the flat 0.2 mile connecting trail to Navajo Loop.

* There is a very steep connecting trail up to Bryce Point that you are skipping so the description, mileage, and difficulty listed on the National Park Service's webpage for Peekaboo Loop Trail are not the same as what you are doing.

Last Section- Navajo Loop Trail
2 choices to hike back to the rim: Wall Street or Two Bridges side of the loop

The left (southern) side of the Loop, Wall Street, climbs 500 ft in 0.7 miles. The right (northern) side, Two Bridges, climbs the same amount in 0.6 miles.

Wall Street is named because it goes through a narrow slot canyon, "Wall Street," which is the only slot canyon in the park. Slot canyons are narrow and therefore often shady so that makes Wall Street our choice for the climb back up.

Two Bridges is nice as well and not that much sunnier so really take your pick. This side is named because there is a small side canyon off of the main trail that has 2 stone arches across it.

Wall Street suffers from erosion and there is a chance of falling rock at any time on the trail. It is usually closed in the winter for this reason.

The majority of the trail on both sides of Navajo Loop consists of switchbacks climbing steeply upwards. We recommend stopping at every second turn to dole out Skittles as well as to make sure everyone is drinking their water. Start promising ice cream at the General Store about halfway up.

The switchbacks coming up Navajo Loop Trail. Steep but thankfully short.

General Trail Information And Advice For The 3 Trail Combo

Some people prefer to start at the steeper Navajo Loop and finish on the more gently ascending Queen's Garden, but we prefer to do the steep switchbacks at the end. For one, the narrow canyon walls of Navajo Trail provide a little shade which is nice when it is getting on towards noon. And two, we find the switchbacks provide a natural stopping place from which to dole out candy in order to bribe weary children uphill.

Dirt in my Shoes blog has a detailed description of the trail combo although she starts at Navajo Loop and ends at Queen's Garden. She has great pictures too.

Start at Queen's Garden at Sunrise Point before 8am in order to finish Navajo Loop at Sunset Point before noon. This is written with summer in mind, where not only do early starts beat the crowds but also the heat. If you are here at another time of year, talk to a Ranger for their advice on when to start.

Peekaboo Loop is also a horse trail so be aware that you must stand to the side to let horses pass and there will be the lovely smell of horse poop on the trail.

Alternative Route- Peekaboo And Queen's Garden Trail Only
4.8 miles long and plan about 2.5 hours to hike

Start at Bryce Point and hike down to Peekaboo Loop (1.1 miles) and take the west, (left fork from this direction) going past the Cathedral and Wall of Windows (1.7 miles). Take the connecting trail to Queen's Garden (0.2 miles) and exit that way (1.8 miles) to Sunrise Point.

Take the shuttle back to your car and call it a day. Do the entire Navajo Loop (1.3 miles) on the first afternoon you are here so you don't miss it. (Or in the evening if you are here in the summer.)

Lunch Day 5

Head to the Lodge for lunch at its restaurant or go to Valhalla Pizza.

Or walk to the General Store for some sandwiches and that promised ice cream. You can hop on the shuttle bus from Sunset Point if you don't feel like walking. It is just under a mile from Sunset Point to the General Store along the Rim Trail or 2 stops on the northbound shuttle from Sunset Point to the stop between Sunrise Point and the General Store.

Afternoon and Evening Day 5
Relax and Stargazing

Read a book, take a nap, or do a kids program with the Rangers. Walk to the General Store for another ice cream during the afternoon. Have a later dinner at the Lodge or Valhalla Pizza.

Stay up late to participate in one of the astronomy programs that include an hour long, multimedia talk by a ranger on their favorite astronomy subject. Then everyone has a chance to look through the park's powerful telescope.

There are also amazing full moon hikes if you are lucky enough to be here during a full moon. The park offers these hikes year-round as the rangers will do them on snowshoes in the winter. The hikes during the summer are only 1-2 miles long but descend into the canyon. No children under 6 allowed.

Hanging out on the front porch of the General Store in Bryce Canyon

Day 6

Day Trip to Grand Staircase- Escalante National Monument and Kodachrome Basin State Park

The Plan

- ❖ Sleep in a little compared to yesterday

- ❖ Hike the beautiful and fun for everyone Willis Creek Slot Canyon in Grand Staircase- Escalante National Monument

- ❖ Have lunch at IDK BBQ in Cannonville before exploring Kodachrome Basin State Park in the afternoon and evening

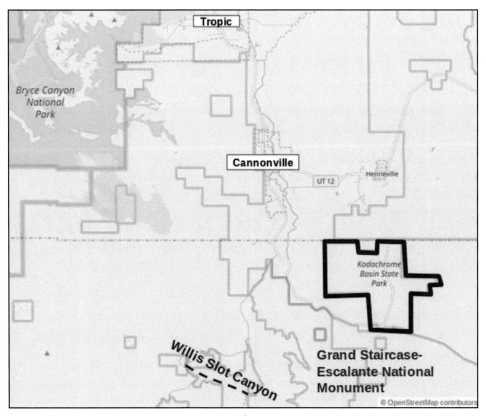

Map of Day 6

Morning Day 6
Willis Creek Slot Canyon

Willis Creek is a fantastic slot canyon in Grand Staircase- Escalante National Monument. Think of it as a miniaturized Narrows, except that you can hop over the water and the walls are just an arm length apart at times. It is a photographer's dream because of the lines of erosion on the curvy canyon walls. While you are busy snapping photos, the kids will be busy skipping through the creek having a blast.

It takes some effort to get to the trailhead but it is well worth it. This is a showstopper of a hike that is doable for all ages. Aim to be here around mid to late morning, meaning you will be leaving Bryce around 930am.

Directions to Willis Creek Slot Canyon
(50 min/ 26 miles from Bryce Canyon Lodge)

Head back out to Hwy 12 from Bryce Canyon and turn right. After you pass through Tropic, continue 5 miles until you see a KOA on your right. You are now in Cannonville. Turn right onto Main Street by the Grand Staircase Inn, following the signs for Kodachrome Basin State Park and the Visitor Center for Grand Staircase-Escalante National Monument.

The nice, new **Visitor Center** for Grand Staircase-Escalante is a block down Main St and is a good place to stop for current weather information (cell signal is iffy sometimes). They have a cool topographic model of the whole monument and some early pioneer artifacts. The rangers are very helpful and will tell you of any road conditions you need to know, a definite plus because once you are out there, you are on your own. The Visitor Center is closed mid- November through mid-March and open M-F 8am-430pm otherwise.

Get back on Main St (also called Cottonwood Canyon Rd) and head south for almost 3 miles until you see a wooden sign pointing right for Skutumpah Road. Turn right on this graded, dirt road. It is also marked as BLM 500 on some maps.

It is dirt road for the next 6 miles to the Willis Creek trailhead, but the road is in good shape. We managed it in a loaded minivan. That being said, we would not have attempted it without 4WD if it was at all muddy. (And even then maybe not. The clay around here has reputation for being super slick when it is wet, no matter what you are driving.)

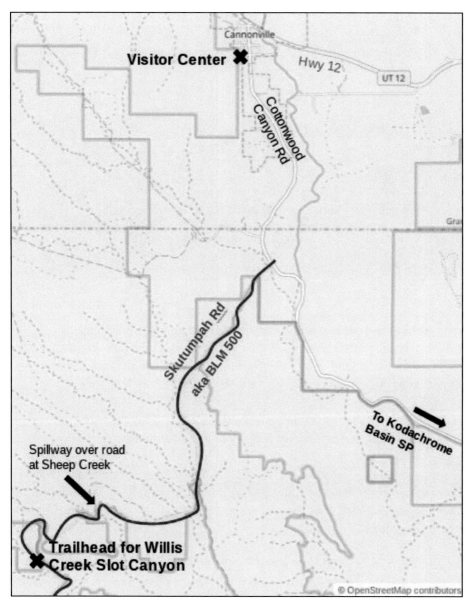

Map of Willis Creek Slot Canyon Trailhead

For evidence that driving in the rain would be a bad idea; there is a large hill almost immediately after you turn on Skutumpah Road that would be terrible to try in the mud.

Big hill on Skutumpah Road

You are now in Grand Staircase- Escalante National Monument and it is as beautiful as it is desolate. You can see the cliffs of Bryce Canyon in the distance on the right side of the car and you can imagine the Grand Canyon in the distance on the other side of the car. The views go on forever.

After awhile, there is a dam/ retaining wall over Sheep Creek where the spillway is over the road. This would be difficult if the water level was high.

After your second creek crossing (most likely dry in the summer), look for Willis Creek Slot Canyon Trailhead on your right. You won't miss it, it is a large parking area and it is well- signed. You cross the road to start the trail on the opposite side from the parking lot.

It takes 20- 30 min to drive this 6 mile, dirt road section, depending on the road conditions. There are smaller roads appearing on both sides, mostly unmarked or marked with BLM #'s. Ignore them and stay on Skutumpah/ BLM 500.

You can see Bryce Canyon in the distance from Skutumpah Road

Willis Creek Slot Canyon
2- 4.2 miles RT, expect to spend 1-2 hours

This is an easy, flat trail and you even get to walk into the slot canyon, no hard climbs down. The most scenic section is in the first mile which is why it is so popular. Minimal effort (aside from the drive) is needed to get to superb scenery.

The trail is 2.1 miles long to the confluence with Sheep Creek but most people turn around at the junction with Averett Canyon (1 mile) because that is where the narrows end. After that, the trail to Sheep Creek is pretty but nothing spectacular.

From the parking lot, cross the road and follow the trail through the scrub for 0.1 miles until it leads to the creek. Start walking along the creek bed through the canyon. The water is usually only 4-6 inches high but is almost always present, nice on a hot day.

Alternatively you can hop right in the creek from the parking lot and do a bit of rock scrambling until the creek meets the trail and the way becomes easier.

The first set of narrows along the trail is great but it is the second set that really will knock your socks off. The walls are only 6 feet apart here and 100 ft high. The erosion lines on the side and the shadows from the sun made for some amazing pictures. We spent most of our time here. The kids loved the curvy walls and splashing in the stream.

Averett Canyon is easily identified when it joins Willis Creek. You can only explore it a very short distance though as there is a humongous boulder blocking the way.

From this point it is another mile to the confluence with Sheep Creek but there are no more spectacular narrows. The canyon walls are still high though, and beautiful colors of red and orange. Hike for as long as you want, then turn around.

We hiked a little beyond Averett Canyon for a 2.6 mile RT hike that took us about 80 min. There was lots of stopping for pictures and splashing in water.

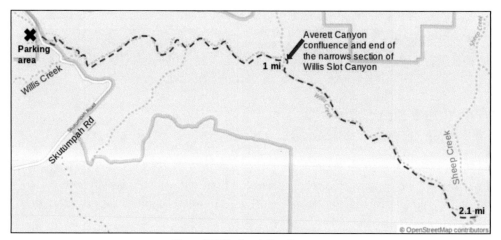

Map of Willis Creek Slot Canyon

Advice For Hiking Willis Creek Slot Canyon

Wear water shoes such as Keens. Part of the fun of this trail is being able to splash in the water so let the kids go for it.

There are no toilets at the parking area but there is also no one around so it isn't that big of a problem.

Bring water, food, and sunscreen. Although the narrows sections are nice and shady, there are sections where the trail opens up and it can be very sunny.

Check in with the Visitor Center to get a weather update before you go. **This is a slot canyon so flash floods are always possible**, especially on summer afternoons when it thunderstorms like clockwork.

Get a road update at the Visitor Center as well. You do not want to find out there were road issues after you start driving on Skutumpah Road because there will be no one around to help. Again, we managed just fine in a loaded Kia Sedona so the road is definitely doable. It is well maintained and graded. Just please be aware that it can quickly become impassable. Do not take it if it is raining or about to rain. This trail is usually inaccessible in winter.

If one of the kids gets disgustingly dirty on the hike, you can drive over to Kodachrome Basin SP afterwards and use the showers there for a small fee.

Have a blast with your camera and your filters in Willis Creek Slot Canyon

One of the more open sections of the trail along Willis Creek

Lunch Day 6

Drive out to I.D.K BBQ in the parking lot of the Grand Staircase Inn in Cannonville and enjoy some tasty food. If the food truck isn't there or you don't like bbq, drive 5 miles up to Tropic and have lunch at the Pizzeria or Rustler's Restaurant.

Or plan ahead and bring a picnic to enjoy at Kodachrome Basin State Park.

Afternoon Day 6
Kodachrome Basin State Park

Kodachrome was an unexpected find that we only discovered as we were looking for a place to camp near Bryce Canyon. It turned out to be a very happy surprise.

The park is small but crowd-free, well run, and has fantastically large monoliths that geologists are not entirely sure how were formed. These sedimentary pipes made for amazing black and white pictures. Consider camping here at least one night at least on your trip as this is one of our favorite campgrounds in the US. If you can't camp, then be sure to make a stop here on your way back from Willis Creek to check out this little gem of a state park.

General Information And Tips About Kodachrome

The 2018 brochure (download it from the website) is excellent, giving a little about the history, geology, flora and fauna of the park as well as good maps of the hikes and points of interest.

It does get hot in the summer so if you want to do one of the longer hikes, wait until late afternoon to start. Or come here first thing in the morning and do Willis Creek Slot Canyon afterwards (if there are no thunderstorms).

Getting to Kodachrome is easy. From Hwy 12, turn onto Main St in Cannonville and stay on that road as it becomes Cottonwood Canyon Rd. About 15 min later you will see a road to the left for Kodachrome Basin SP. Everything is paved, a marked improvement from this morning's adventure.

Looking down on the Basin Campground from Angel's Palace Trail

What to Do in Kodachrome Basin State Park

After paying the $8/ car entrance fee, take a driving tour around while you are waiting for the heat of the afternoon to subside. The park is open 6am- 10pm.

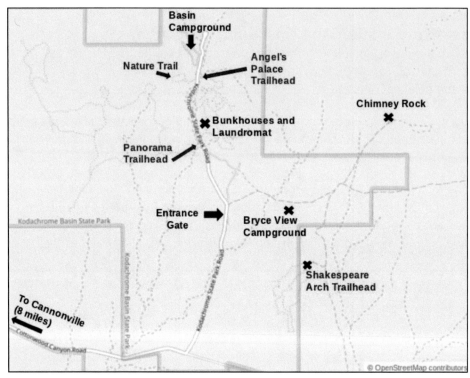

Map of Kodachrome State Park

Driving Tour Of The Park

First, drive north from the entrance gate to the turn-around where the Basin Campground is located. On the way back, look on the right for the trailhead for the Nature Trail.

Nature Trail. This half-mile, paved trail has signs detailing the flora and fauna found in the park. It is easily doable and interesting even on a hot summer afternoon. Wheelchair accessible.

Keep driving back towards the entrance gate but turn left before you get there. The road becomes dirt but it is flat and well- graded. You'll pass by the other, more primitive campground of Bryce View, then take another left, following the signs for Chimney Rock.

Chimney Rock The largest and tallest (at 170ft) of the more than 60 monoliths in the park. This a great black and white photography spot as it sort of stands alone against the flat surroundings.

Black and white photo of Chimney Rock

Drive south from Chimney Rock towards Shakespeare Arch and park the car again.

Shakespeare Arch This is a 1.7 mile loop trail that is difficult at the end but the first 0.5 mile to the Arch is easy so take a stroll there and back. There is no shade though so bring a hat with you and wear sunscreen.

*** If you really like stone arches, then exit the park and drive back out to Cottonwood Canyon Road. Turn left to head east into Grand Staircase- Escalante National Monument. This quickly becomes an unpaved road and all warnings from this morning about wet weather and zero cell phone signals hold true again. 11 miles and 30 min later, you will arrive at **Grosvenor Arch,** an impressive double arch. Best to drive this road in a 4WD with a high clearance. It is a beautiful area though.

Finish The Day With A Sunset Hike
This is very cool as the Estrada rocks turn gorgeous reds and oranges with the setting sun. There are 2 good hikes to watch the sunset from.

1. Panorama: This is the classic hike in Kodachrome and can be done as a 3 or 6 mile loop. There are impressive monoliths, a shallow "cave," and a great overlook. (You skip the "cave" if you only do the 3 mile loop.)

2. Angel's Palace: An easy 1.5 mile loop that climbs up 150 ft to the top of the rocks by Basin Campground. The views are amazing and the kids liked the rock scramble.

View from Angel's Palace at sunset

Day 6 Evening

Dinner and Drive Back to Bryce Canyon National Park

Drive 40 min (24 miles) from Kodachrome back to your lodgings in Bryce Canyon NP. Stop for dinner in Tropic at the halfway mark. Or head to Foster's Family Steakhouse or Bryce Canyon Pines Restaurant a few miles west of Bryce Canyon City on Hwy 12.

Day 7

Return to Las Vegas

Get up early and check out of your lodgings. It is a 4 hour/ 260 mile drive back to Las Vegas from Bryce Canyon National Park. You do not return through Zion NP, instead you head north from Panguitch and cut over to I-15 via Hwy 20. From there it is a straight shot south on I-15. There isn't much in the way of important sights along the way, but the scenery is pretty.

General Tips For Your Trip To Southwest Utah

Always be conscious of the weather, whether it's heat or cold or thunderstorms or snow. Knowing the weather is good advice anywhere, but in Southwest Utah it seems a little more urgent with the real possibility of heat stroke in the summer and flash floods anytime of year.

Do not depend on your cell phone for weather. We have the hardest time getting weather apps or websites to load on phones because of poor cell signals.

Hydrate, hydrate, hydrate! Bring hydration packs for everyone, even the kids. See our blog *7 Gift Ideas That Will Make Your Kids Want To Go Outside* for the packs we bought for the kids after this trip because water bottles did not cut it.

Bring lots of sunscreen, hats, chapstick, sunglasses, and hand lotion because it is very dry and sunny. The altitude at Bryce means you can burn at anytime of year.

Beware of the wildlife! Not just the bears, coyotes, or snakes but also the chipmunks and squirrels. The squirrels at Zion are huge and quite aggressive. And you will see people feeding them, which is why they are so aggressive. Don't be that person. The chipmunks in Bryce are not as aggressive and really kind of cute until they sneak into your backpack. Watch your stuff!

Stay on the trail. There are numerous social trails throughout all of the parks which are distracting, confusing, and terrible for the environment. Much of the land in these parks may look dry and dead but is actually a cryptobiotic crust. This crust contains bacteria that help hold the soil together to prevent erosion while lessening water run-off, therefore allowing things to grow. When you step on it you set it back for decades. Don't be that person.

If you are camping, check your shoes for scorpions and always zip up your tent. The website *My Utah Parks* has a good page about scorpions and rattlesnakes.

Make sure you have plenty of room on your camera because amazing photo opportunities abound in each of these parks.

Periodically check the official websites for closure alerts as storms, fires, maintenance, etc can close trails and sections of the parks for weeks to months suddenly and unexpectedly.

Rainy Day Activities

In Zion National Park

Tour the Visitor Center and admire its state of the art, environmental design.

Hang out at the **Nature Center** (open in the afternoon in the summer) and play games, see the exhibits, or participate in a kids activity.

Tour the **Human History Museum** and learn about Native Americans and early settlers in the area.

Ride the shuttle around. It is free, dry, and has spectacular scenery.

If you don't mind a little rain, hike up to Lower Emerald Pool and see the waterfall which should start really flowing. In fact, waterfalls start showing up everywhere in Zion and all the people are gone so rain can make for a fun day in the park. Just stay out of any trails involving the Virgin River or narrow canyons.

There is a movie theater in Hurricane, 20 miles away, called Coral Cliffs Cinema.

Go souvenir shopping in Springdale.

In Bryce Canyon National Park

Check out the **Visitor Center** and its 20 minute film about the park. Pick up a book while you are there and learn even more about the park's history.

Drive to the south end of the park and see all the viewpoints. The hoodoos in the rain can make for some really cool pictures.

Don't plan on hiking as everything gets covered in red mud and the trails become slick.

There is a movie theater in Panguitch, 40 min away, called the GEM Theater.

Drive to Kodachrome Basin State Park or Red Canyon in Dixie National Forest to escape the rain and spend the day there.

Check out a board game from the front desk of the Lodge and play in the cosy lobby.

Go shopping at the large and fun gift shop in the Lodge.

Books And Movies About Places In This Guide

The Bryce Canyon store at the Visitor Center offers a nice <u>Day Hikers Packet</u> that includes an auto guide with descriptions of all the viewpoints and 2 trail maps; one with trail descriptions and one with flora and fauna listed. All for $8. You can order it online.

Zion National Park makes some its brochures (flora, fauna, wilderness guides) available for free to download from its website. Bryce Canyon does the same on their website.

Deaths and Rescues in Zion National Park by Dave Nally. An interesting look at all the ways you can die in Zion, written by a slot canyoneer and helped out by a member of the Zion Search and Rescue team. It is not gruesome as much as it is informative and reminds you to be alert and to plan ahead. And to always listen to park rangers.

Water, Rock, and Time: The Geologic Story of Zion National Park by Robert L. Eves. A nice layperson's introduction to how water formed Zion Canyon. Gives you a lot to look for when hiking The Narrows.

Zion National Park has a good list of recommended reads on their website while the Bryce Canyon store also carries a nice collection of books about the park, not all of which can be found on Amazon.

Part of *Butch Cassidy and the Sundance Kid* (1969) was filmed in Zion National Park as well as in nearby St. George. Legend has it that the actual Butch Cassidy hid from a posse in the Red Canyon area and there is a trail there named after him. He was born north of Panguitch and spent a lot of time in the area so it's possible.

That's all for this itinerary. Have a blast exploring Southwest Utah! We hope you have as much fun as we do in this remarkable place. Send us your best photo (#simplyawesometrips) and we will happily post it to our Instagram page. (It doesn't have to be from The Narrows.) We love seeing your vacation photos, honest!

To see more photos of the places mentioned in this guidebook- check out the albums labeled "Zion National Park," "Bryce Canyon National Park," "Willis Creek Slot Canyon," and "Kodachrome Basin State Park" on our Facebook page. We have lots more pictures that will help you plan your trip. Please check out all the blogs related to this itinerary on our website also.

If you find an amazing restaurant, lodging, or activity that you think we should include in future editions or simply have a question or comment about anything in this itinerary, we would love to hear from you. Shoot us an email at: info@simplyawesometrips.com.

If you thought this guidebook was great, please take a moment to help fellow travelers find it by adding a review on Amazon. We appreciate it.

Happy Trails and Safe Travels!

Amy & Amanda

A Thank You Gift!

As a thank you for your purchase, we invite you to visit our website at www.simplyawesometrips.com to purchase a detailed trip itinerary to a destination of your choice for just $5. Use code ZION2019. The offer is good for one itinerary from our website only (pdf format) and expires at the end of 2019.

Our goal is to help you plan a fantastic trip for you and your family!

Additional Titles about National Parks and Other Destinations Available on Amazon and Our Website

  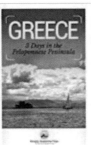  

And More!

Disclosures

At the founding of Simply Awesome Trips, we agreed to travel as we always have with our families—on our own dime. No free nights, no comped visits, not even any swag. We continue to feel good about that decision.

We do participate in affiliate marketing with some of the companies that we personally use (Booking.com, VRBO.com). They don't pay us to write, we simply get a commission if you enter those sites through our "gate" as opposed to say a Google search. But we also recommend lodging, restaurants, and activities where we don't receive any commission, such as Airbnb or private rental agencies. If it's good; it's good. We don't change our recommendations based on vendor.

All maps courtesy of OpenStreetMap. www.openstreetmap.org/copyright.

Liability Statement

Although the author has made every effort to ensure that the information in this itinerary was correct at the time of publishing, the author does not assume and hereby disclaims any liability to any party for any loss, damage, or disruption caused by errors or omissions, whether such errors or omissions result from negligence, accident, or any other cause. The authors, publishers, and contributors to this itinerary, either directly or indirectly, disclaim any liability for injuries, accidents, and damages, whatsoever that may occur to those using this guide. You are responsible for your health and safety for all aspects of this itinerary. Be safe and use good judgment.

By providing links to other sites, Simply Awesome Trips does not guarantee, approve, or endorse, the information or products available on these sites.

Made in the USA
Middletown, DE
28 March 2023

27828365R00044